Preparing the Table of the Word

Normand Bonneau, OMI

NOVALIS
THE LITURGICAL PRESS

Design: Eye-to-Eye Design, Toronto

Layout: Suzanne Latourelle

Illustrations: Eugene Kral

Series Editor: Bernadette Gasslein

© 1997, Novalis, Saint Paul University, Ottawa, Ontario, Canada

Business Office: Novalis, 49 Front Street East, 2nd floor, Toronto, Ontario M5E 1B3

Published in the United States of America by The Liturgical Press, Box 7500, Collegeville, MN 56321-7500

Novalis: ISBN 2-89088-794-4

The Liturgical Press: ISBN 0-8146-2499-5
    A Liturgical Press Book
    Library of Congress data available on request.

Printed in Canada.

Canadian Cataloguing in Publication Data

Bonneau, Normand, 1948–
    Preparing the table of the Word

(Preparing for liturgy)
Includes bibliographical references.

    1. Word of God (Theology). 2. Bible — Liturgical use.
    3. Catholic Church — Liturgy. I. Title. II. Series

BX2003.B64 1997   264'.02   C97-900706-2

Contents

Introduction

Preparing the table of the word: in the context of liturgy, "preparing a table" would naturally evoke preparing the eucharistic table, for, when the people of God celebrate the eucharist, they offer, bless, break and share the gifts of bread and wine transformed into the body and blood of Christ. What does the phrase "the table of the word" mean, then?

Transferring language that is normally used for the eucharistic table and applying it to the scriptures suggests that the word of God, like bread and wine, is a source of life and nourishment. The use of food images to describe the word of God is not new. In the gospel, Jesus, replying to the devil who was tempting him to assuage his hunger by turning stones into bread, cites a passage from Israel's ancient scriptures: "One does not live by bread alone, but by every word that comes from the mouth of God" (Deuteronomy 8:3, cited in Matthew 4:4). The Lord himself found nourishment at the table of God's word during his forty-day fast in the desert.

Weaving the same images in a slightly different way, the authors of Vatican II's *Dogmatic Constitution on Divine Revelation* composed the phrases that inspired the title of this book:

> *The church has always held the divine scriptures in reverence no less than it accords to the Lord's body itself, never ceasing—especially in the sacred liturgy—to receive the bread of life from the one table of God's word and Christ's body, and to offer it to the faithful (21).*

As the document states, the church offers nourishment from one table, a nourishment that takes two forms: the word of God and the body of Christ. The Constitution's play of images is not a mere flight of fancy. In placing both Christ's body and God's word on the same liturgical table, the Council document implies that what is said of one can be said of the other. As a consequence, the reverence with which we surround the body of Christ applies equally to God's word, especially when this word is proclaimed in the liturgy. If we hold the same reverence for God's word proclaimed in the liturgy as we do for the sacrament of the eucharist, then by implication the proclamation of God's word is, like the eucharist, sacramental—it effects Christ's saving presence.

This is precisely what another Vatican II document declares. In describing the different facets of Christ's presence at the eucharistic celebration, the *Constitution on the Sacred Liturgy* (*CSL*) explains that Christ

> ... *is always present to his church, especially during the liturgy. (...) He is present through the sacrifice which is the mass, at once in the person of the minister, (...) and also, most fully, under the eucharistic elements. (...)* He is present through his word, in that he himself is speaking when scripture is read in church (*7, emphasis added*).

In liturgical proclamation, the words of scripture become Word, that is, they become Jesus himself speaking here and now. The Constitution makes no distinction as to whether the passage being read is from the Old Testament, the apostolic writings, or the gospels—as long as scripture is being read, Christ is speaking. Liturgical proclamation of the scriptures makes Christ present, he who comes in our midst to transform us more and more into the saving mystery of his death and resurrection. Something ineffable is happening when we assemble for the liturgy of the word. All the more reason, then, to prepare our celebrations well.

How do we prepare to celebrate at the table of God's word? *The Introduction to the Lectionary for Mass* (LM) provides the necessary guidelines. Published in 1981 as an elaborated revision of an earlier 1969 edition, it is included at the front of most editions of the Lectionary. The LM is a mine of information. Anyone wishing to know about the liturgy of the word will find this document well worth consulting. Here, we will be concerned first and foremost with what the document says about *preparing* to celebrate at the table of God's word.

Two Types of Preparation

In general, the document speaks of two types of preparation, a *spiritual* preparation and a *technical* preparation. While the technical preparation concerns more immediately those whose task is to proclaim the readings and preach the homily, spiritual preparation, which the document subdivides into *biblical* and *liturgical,* applies to everyone. Preparing to celebrate at the table of God's word means gaining familiarity with the scriptures and with the way the liturgy uses the scriptures, particularly through the Lectionary.

In Summary

1. The church nourishes us at the one table of God's word and Christ's body.

2. When the scriptures are proclaimed in the liturgical assembly, Christ is speaking.

3. There are two types of preparation for celebrating at the table of God's word: spiritual, which entails a biblical aspect and a liturgical aspect (for everyone), and technical (for lectors and presiders).

Discussion Questions

1. Do you expect anything to happen in the liturgy of the word?

2. How in the liturgy do we show reverence for the eucharist?

3. How in the liturgy do we show reverence for the word of God?

CHAPTER 1

The Liturgy of the Word

What is the liturgy of the word? What are the elements composing it? What is its purpose? Who must perform what functions for its celebration?

Along with the liturgy of the eucharist (see *Preparing the Eucharistic Table* in this series), the liturgy of the word is one of the two major components of the mass. The LM explains the relationship between word and eucharist in this way:

> The Church is nourished spiritually at the table of God's word and at the table of the eucharist: from the one it grows in wisdom and from the other in holiness. In the word of God the divine covenant is announced; in the eucharist the new and everlasting covenant is renewed. The spoken word of God brings to mind the history of salvation; the eucharist embodies it in the sacramental signs of the liturgy (10).

The document then goes on to say that the table of God's word and the table of the eucharist form "one single act of divine worship"—no word without sacrament, no sacrament without word. The liturgy of the word, then, is not a mere appendage, but an integral part of the eucharistic liturgy.

The liturgy of the word is composed of several elements. The LM enumerates seven: biblical readings (nos. 12-18); responsorial psalm (nos. 19-22); acclamation before the reading of the gospel (no. 23); homily (nos. 24-27); silence (no. 28); profession of faith (no. 29); general intercessions (nos. 30-31).

Purpose

In essence, the liturgy of the word is a dialogue between God and the assembled community. This dialogue takes place in several modalities. When the readings are proclaimed, and in the moments of silence interspersed throughout, the assembly listens to and ponders God's word. The responsorial psalm, as its name indicates, invites the assembly to respond to the word it has heard. This is usually done by the assembly singing the refrain, which highlights a particular aspect of the first reading, while the cantor chants the verses. After the second reading, the assembly honours and welcomes Christ in the gospel by standing to sing the gospel acclamation. The homily proclaims the word by interpreting it and showing how it is at work transforming the assembly and the world into the pattern of the paschal mystery. After a period of quiet reflection, the assembly responds by reciting the creed. Finally, the assembly exercises its priestly role by offering to God prayers for the church, the world, and all creation.

Roles

Three interrelated roles—the assembly, the presider and the lector(s)—express the dialogue between the two partners. The LM addresses each of these roles in turn. In this book, we focus primarily on what the document says about the kind of *preparation* needed for each to perform its function.

One important element in this dialogue merits attention: the place and role of silence.

> *The dialogue between God and [God's] people taking place through the Holy Spirit demands short intervals of silence, suited to the assembly, as an opportunity to take the word of God to heart and to prepare a response to it in prayer.*
>
> *Proper times for silence during the liturgy of the word are, for example, before this liturgy begins, after the first and the second reading, after the homily (28).*

A moment of silence to let everyone settle before beginning the first reading as well as before the homily, particularly since the people are changing from a standing to a sitting posture, is also recommended.

The assembly

Everything the LM urges of the assembly applies to presiders and lectors as well, for they too are part of the people of God:

> Love of the Scriptures *is therefore the force that renews the entire people of God. All the faithful without exception must therefore always be ready to listen gladly to God's word. When this word is proclaimed in the Church and put into living practice, it enlightens the faithful through the working of the Holy Spirit and draws them into the entire mystery of the Lord as a reality to be lived* (47).
>
> [The faithful are] *to take part attentively, and to dispose themselves to hear the word,* especially by learning beforehand more about Scripture. *That same connection should also awaken in them a desire for a* liturgical understanding of the texts read *and for the willingness to respond through singing* (48; *emphases added*).

I have marked the most important phrases of this passage in Roman type face, for they express in slightly different ways the two aspects of spiritual preparation necessary for celebrating the liturgy of the word—love of the scriptures and an appreciation of their liturgical use.

The presider

For the presider, the LM elaborates:

> *The first requirement for one who is to preside over the celebration is a* thorough knowledge of the structure of the Order of Readings *so that he [or she] will know how to inspire good effects in the hearts of the faithful. Through study and prayer he [or she] must also develop a full understanding of the coordination and connection of the various texts in the liturgy of the word, so that the Order of Readings will become the source of a sound understanding of the mystery of Christ and his saving work* (39).

Above and beyond familiarity with and love of the scriptures, the presider, given the leadership role he or she assumes, should know the Lectionary and its structure thoroughly. Indeed, a good knowledge of the Lectionary should be required of lectors as well, for it is the liturgical book given over to their special care. The assembly might also greatly profit from such knowledge. Therefore, the two aspects of spiritual preparation—love and knowledge of the scriptures, and familiarity with the Lectionary—pertain to all three roles, assembly, presider and lector.

The lector

Before specifying the more technical aspects of the lector's preparation, the LM mentions the same love of the scriptures it has already urged for the assembly and for the presider:

> *Their preparation must above all be* spiritual, *but what may be called technical preparation is also needed. The spiritual preparation presupposes at least a* biblical *and* liturgical *formation. The purpose of their* biblical formation *is to give readers the ability to understand the readings in context and to perceive by the light of faith the central point of the revealed message. The* liturgical formation *ought to equip the readers to have some grasp of the meaning and structure of the liturgy of the word and of the significance of its connection with the liturgy of the eucharist (emphases added).*

Only then does the LM go on to speak of the specific skills required of the lector:

> *The technical preparation should make the readers more skilled in the* art of reading publicly, *either with the power of their own voice or with the help of sound equipment (55; emphasis added).*

Thus, the technical preparation concerns more particularly presiders and lectors who proclaim the word.

In the remainder of this book, we will look at each of these three types of preparation in turn. What does the first aspect of spiritual preparation, love and knowledge of the scriptures, which applies to all three roles, entail? This is the topic of the next chapter.

In Summary

1. The liturgy of the word is a dialogue between God and God's people.

2. The purpose of the liturgy of the word is to make present God's saving act in Christ, who shapes us into his paschal mystery.

3. The three main roles in celebrating the liturgy of the word are the assembly, the presider, and the lector.

Discussion Questions

1. If the liturgy of the word is a dialogue, what is being said between the two partners?

2. How does each of the seven elements contribute to this dialogue?

3. There are three functions in the liturgy of the word. In terms of the dialogue between God and God's people, who speaks in whose name?

CHAPTER 2

Loving and Knowing the Scriptures

The LM insists that the most important preparation one can have for celebrating at the table of God's word is a love and knowledge of the scriptures, which the people of God have always held in highest esteem. The *Dogmatic Constitution on Divine Revelation* explains the role of the scripture in the scheme of God's revelation in this way:

> *The pattern of this revelation unfolds through deeds and words bound together by an inner dynamism, in such a way that God's works, effected during the course of the history of salvation, show forth and confirm the doctrine and the realities signified by the words, while the words in turn proclaim the works and throw light on the meaning hidden in them. By this revelation the truth, both about God and about the salvation of humankind, inwardly dawns on us in Christ, who is in himself both the mediator and the fullness of all revelation (2).*

Words and deeds go hand in hand. Deeds alone, even God's deeds, remain orphans unless they are told and interpreted, while the deeds confirm the words. The scriptures describe, explain and announce the meaning of God's saving actions on behalf of humankind under the thrall of sin and death. They identify us as the holy people of God. The scriptures inspire our imaginations to see the world and ourselves through God's eyes so that we come to realize that the current chapter of the story of salvation is taking place in us and through us. And since for us Christians salvation history finds its culmination in

Christ, loving and knowing the scriptures means loving and knowing Christ. *Liturgical* proclamation of the scriptures intensifies all of this. It is Christ who calls us forth to gather as the people of God. It is Christ, speaking through the scriptures, who is present in our midst, imperceptibly transforming our lives into the mystery of his death and resurrection. It is Christ who invites us to offer with him praise and thanks to God at the table of the eucharist.

Liturgy and Scripture

There are two further reasons for loving and knowing the scriptures as a way of enhancing our liturgical celebrations at the table of God's word. First, the liturgy and the scriptures are so intimately linked that one cannot exist without the other. Secondly, the content and structure of the Lectionary presuppose familiarity with the scriptures.

The scriptures and the liturgy have always been so intimately interrelated that it is nearly impossible to speak of one without speaking of the other. As A.G. Martimort has so aptly noted, "the Bible and the liturgy show the same attitude of human beings to God, the same vision of the world and interpretation of history, so much so that there can be no liturgical life without an introduction to the Bible, while the liturgy in turn provides the Bible with a living commentary that enables it to manifest its full meaning"(in *The Church at Prayer: An Introduction to the Liturgy, Vol. 1: Principles of the Liturgy,* 140).

Liturgy and Bible interact as reciprocal sources. Many passages, such as psalms, hymns, canticles, have liturgy as their source and setting. Liturgical practices have shaped key foundational narratives like the Passover (Exodus 12:1-13:6), the revelation of the covenant on Sinai (Exodus 19-24), the conquest of the promised land (Joshua, esp. chapter 6), the baptism of Jesus and the Last Supper in the gospels—to name only the most obvious. In yet other instances, liturgical concerns have left traces on the composition of entire books, for example, Joshua and Deuteronomy. Finally, liturgical use in synagogue and church determined which books would be included in the Old and New Testaments.

In turn, the Bible is one of the main sources of liturgy. The *Constitution on the Sacred Liturgy* explains: "The importance of scripture in the celebration of the liturgy is paramount. For it is texts from scripture that form the readings and are explained in the homily; it is scripture's psalms that are sung; from scripture's inspiration and influence flow the various kinds of prayers as well as the singing in the liturgy; from scripture the actions and signs derive their meaning" (24). The eucharistic prayers, as well as most prefaces, are pastiches of scriptural texts and allusions. The Easter blessing of baptismal water is a long rehearsal of God's mighty acts in salvation history. Even an incidental prayer such as that voiced by the assembly before receiving communion ("Lord, I am not worthy to receive you, but only say the word and I shall be healed") is adapted from the words of the centurion whose son (or servant) Jesus heals (Matthew 8:8 = Luke 7:6). Thus the scriptures and the liturgy form the warp and woof of the tapestry of our Christian lives.

Structure of the Lectionary

In addition, knowledge of the scriptures becomes all the more necessary for celebrating at the table of God's word because of the nature and structure of the Lectionary, a topic we will discuss at length in the next chapters 3 and 4. Suffice it to say here that the *Sunday and Feast Day Lectionary* contains only 13% of the Bible. It is highly selective, choosing passages as they suit liturgical seasons and their patterns. Moreover, the "pericopic" approach (*pericope* comes from two Greek words—*peri*, which means "around," and *koptein* meaning "to cut"; hence, passages cut out) results in biblical selections being taken out of their original contexts.

As a result, the Lectionary presupposes that worshippers are familiar with the overall story line of the Bible and that they can situate, in a general way, the readings proclaimed at the Sunday eucharist in their biblical and historical settings.

Learning to Know and Love the Scriptures

How does one learn to love and know the scriptures? Praying and private reading of the scriptures immediately come to mind, but often people who try this approach without some initiation and guidance easily become discouraged. Usually it is wiser to avail oneself of biblical courses, sessions and workshops, and to read articles and books by reputable and knowledgeable scholars. Consulting parish and diocesan personnel can usually surface the resources available locally.

While parishes and dioceses often offer courses, workshops, and conferences on scripture and liturgy, opportunities to learn about the Lectionary are few and far between. Thus, chapter 3 will examine the principles underlying the choice of biblical passages in the Lectionary, while chapter 4 provides an overview of the patterns that give shape to the Lectionary's way of articulating the various liturgical seasons.

In Summary

1. Loving and knowing the scriptures means loving and knowing Christ.

2. The scriptures and the liturgy weave the tapestry of our Christian lives.

3. The Lectionary, the church's main liturgical appropriation of the scriptures, has a structure.

Discussion Questions

1. Can you think of other ways the Bible and the liturgy are related?

2. What resources for bible study—people, books, programs—exist in your area?

CHAPTER 3

Nature and Structure of the Lectionary

First promulgated by Pope Paul VI on May 29, 1969, and slightly revised in 1981, the *Sunday and Feast Day Lectionary* stands as one of the highlights of the Vatican II liturgical reform. Never before in the history of liturgy had such a thorough and informed revision of a Lectionary been done.

The Lectionary and the Paschal Mystery

Permeating the entire Lectionary lies a principle so fundamental that, although not immediately obvious, it colours every aspect of the selection and distribution of the biblical readings contained in it. The *Sunday and Feast Day Lectionary* is entirely oriented to the paschal mystery of Christ. It is designed, not primarily for catechetical purposes, or as a source of doctrinal instruction, or as a pageant of the sweep of salvation history, or as a chronological retelling of the life of Jesus, or as a guide for moral life. Its aim is "to proclaim the passion, death, and resurrection of Christ, fully realized in him and being realized in us who, through faith and baptism, have been joined to him" (William Skudlarek, *The Word in Worship: Preaching in a Liturgical Context* [Nashville: Abingdon, 1981], 34). Embedded within the church's weekly celebration of the Sunday eucharist, the Lectionary shapes and molds us into the people of God, the body of Christ.

Because the Lectionary represents the church's *liturgical* use of scripture, liturgical principles take precedence over exegesis, catechesis, exhortation or other concerns in determining the selection and distribution of biblical passages in the Sunday Lectionary. If this is so, what is liturgy all about that it so totally influences the Lectionary?

Building the Story of Salvation

Liturgy celebrates in ritual form the saving relationship between the risen Lord and the assembled community. This saving relationship takes the pattern of the paschal mystery of his death and resurrection through which we are being created anew. Every death and rebirth that marks our lives configures us more and more into the likeness of Christ, crucified and risen. By walking us through the different seasons of the liturgical year, the liturgy helps us understand and deepen the different "seasons" of our lives and build them into a story of salvation. The season of Lent, for example, tells the story of the paschal mystery as conversion and repentance, culminating in our passage through death to new life through baptism and eucharist at the Easter Vigil. The Easter season celebrates the story of our deepening communion with the risen Lord who abides with his church through the Spirit, and offers a foretaste of the heavenly banquet of God's reign. The Advent-Christmas season unfolds the story of our patient waiting for the fullness of the kingdom still to come, a time of commemoration and anticipation which we fill with purposeful action until the fullness of the paschal mystery is revealed in us. By telling the story of Jesus' public ministry, the Sundays in Ordinary Time pace us along the difficult fidelity of discipleship.

In each instance, the readings selected for the Sunday Lectionary articulate and celebrate the story of our lives in light of the saving story of Jesus. That is why the Sunday eucharist, which celebrates the paschal mystery, and the liturgical year, every aspect of which flows from and points to the paschal mystery of Christ, together fully determine the design and content of the Sunday Lectionary.

Architecture of the Sunday Lectionary

The *Sunday and Feast Day Lectionary* achieves this paschal design in great part through its carefully configured structure:

- It is organized in a three-year cycle, with Matthew's gospel assigned to Year A, Mark's gospel to Year B, and Luke's gospel to Year C. John's gospel has a special place during the seasons of Lent and Easter.

- Each Sunday and each feast of the Lord contains three readings, the first from the Old Testament, the second from the New Testament apostolic writings, the third from the gospels. During the season of Easter, an excerpt from the Acts of the Apostles replaces the Old Testament as first reading.

- For the Sundays and feast days of the festal seasons of Advent, Christmas, Lent and Easter, the biblical passages are for the most part selected to express the main themes of the season.

- The Sundays in Ordinary Time exhibit their own distribution patterns: both the second reading from the apostolic writings and the third reading from the gospels follow a pattern of semicontinuous reading, while the first reading from the Old Testament is selected to correspond with the gospel passage of the day.

- As a response to the first reading, the Lectionary assigns a psalm to be sung by the cantor and the congregation. Before the gospel proclamation, the Lectionary places an acclamation which is generally gleaned from the scriptures.

In turn, this structure comes about through the Lectionary's use of a number of principles of reading selection and of patterns of reading distribution:

- *Harmony* is the principle whereby the liturgy selects scriptural books or passages that best articulate the main theme or themes of a festal season or a feast.

- *Thematic groupings* are patterns in which biblical readings are organized within a festal season.

- *Semicontinuous reading*, a modern adaptation of the ancient practice of *lectio continua* or continuous reading, is the sequential reading of a biblical book, all the while skipping certain verses or passages.

- *Correspondence* refers to the thematic relationship between two or among all three readings of a Sunday or feast day celebration.

Different combinations of these give each liturgical season its own profile. The liturgical year (see *Preparing the Liturgical Year 1: Sunday and the Easter Triduum*, and *Preparing the Liturgical Year 2: Lent-Easter and Advent-Christmas* in this series) is made up of two types of liturgical season, festal seasons (Advent, Christmas, Lent and Easter) and ordinary time (from the end of the Christmas season to the beginning of Lent, resuming after Pentecost to the beginning of the following Advent). The Lectionary reflects the distinction between the two types of seasons by using *harmony, thematic groupings,* and *correspondence* for the festal seasons, and *semicontinuous reading* and a more limited form of correspondence (between the first and third readings only) for the Sundays in Ordinary Time. The particular shape of each individual season in the Lectionary is the topic of the next chapter. Appreciating these underlying principles of reading selection and patterns of reading distribution will help all who exercise liturgical ministries prepare liturgical celebrations on the scale of entire seasons rather than simply from one Sunday to the next.

In Summary

1. The *Sunday and Feast Day Lectionary* is entirely oriented to the paschal mystery of Christ.

2. The readings for each liturgical season, for each Sunday, and for each feast day of the Lord articulate and celebrate the story of our lives in light of the saving story of Jesus.

3. For each liturgical season, the Lectionary uses different combinations of four principles: harmony, thematic groupings, semicontinuous reading, and correspondence.

Discussion Questions

1. How do people in your community live out the paschal mystery of Christ's death and resurrection? How does the liturgy help us all in this journey?

2. From your experience, what would you say are the strengths and weaknesses of the Sunday Lectionary?

3. How do people in your community experience their own stories as part of the great story of salvation they hear proclaimed Sunday after Sunday, season after season?

CHAPTER 4

The Sunday Lectionary: Principles and Patterns

The *Sunday and Feast Day Lectionary* is not an arbitrary collection of biblical excerpts. The passages are selected with specific aims in mind, aims that the liturgy determines. Below is a brief summary of the key principles of reading selection and the most important patterns of reading distribution for each season. Their order follows the presentation found in another most useful document, the *General Norms for the Liturgical Year and the Calendar (GNLYC)*. Rather than list the seasons chronologically beginning with Advent, this document starts with the Easter Triduum, the very heart of the liturgical year, and then proceeds to consider the seasons as they unfold the paschal mystery—Easter, Lent, Christmas, Advent and Ordinary Time. In fact, this is the sequence in which the festal seasons developed historically.

The Easter Triduum

Christ redeemed us all and gave perfect glory to God principally through his paschal mystery: dying he destroyed our death and rising he restored our life. Therefore the Easter triduum of the passion and resurrection of Christ is the culmination of the entire liturgical year. Thus the solemnity of Easter has the same kind of preeminence in the liturgical year that Sunday has in the week.

The Easter triduum begins with the evening Mass of the Lord's Supper, reaches its high point in the Easter vigil, and closes with evening prayer on Easter Sunday (GNLYC, 18 and 19).

The Easter Triduum is one solemn feast extended over three days that are calculated liturgically, that is, from sundown to sundown. The first day begins at the evening Mass of the Lord's Supper on Thursday and concludes after the celebration of the Lord's Passion on Friday. The second day stretches from sundown Friday to sundown Saturday. The final day embraces the Easter Vigil and Easter morning, coming to a close at Sunday evening prayer.

For this most solemn time of the liturgical year, the Lectionary selects the choicest biblical passages according to the principle of harmony. The Triduum is so very much one feast that correspondence permeates the readings through the three days.

Harmony	Yes. Special books: Exodus, John's gospel
Thematic groupings	Old Testament at Easter Vigil
Semicontinuous reading	None
Correspondence	Extensively throughout the entire Triduum

Mass of the Lord's Supper

Exodus 12:1-8, 11-14: Instructions for the first Passover meal; 1 Corinthians 11:23-26: Paul's account of Jesus' words over bread and wine; John 13:1-15: Jesus washes his disciples' feet.

These readings proclaim the paschal mystery in a rich tapestry of images. The gospel of Jesus washing his disciples' feet narrates an enacted parable of Jesus giving his life for his friends. By citing Jesus' words over the bread and wine at the last supper, Paul exhorts the Corinthians to give of themselves in service to each other. The Exodus account of the people of Israel preparing the passover lamb on the eve of their liberation through the Red Sea provides the matrix for interpreting the passing over of Christ from death to new life.

Celebration of the Lord's Passion

> *Isaiah 52:13-53:12: The Song of the Suffering Servant;*
> *Hebrews 4:14-16; 5:7-9: Christ learned obedience through*
> *suffering; John 18:1-19:42: The Passion.*

The crucifixion of Jesus authenticates what the last supper symbolically prefigured: Jesus loving his own to the end. The high point of this liturgical celebration lies in the solemn proclamation of the Passion according to John. From earliest Christian liturgical tradition, this narrative has held preeminent place at the annual commemoration of Jesus' death and resurrection. The excerpt from the Letter to the Hebrews interprets Jesus' execution on the cross as *the* perfect sacrifice, Jesus as *the* high priest. The first reading from Isaiah, the Fourth Song of the Suffering Servant, uncannily foreshadows the paschal mystery of Jesus' death and resurrection.

Resurrection of the Lord—Easter Vigil

> *Genesis 1:1-2:2: The Creation; Genesis 22:1-18: The sacrifice*
> *of Isaac; Exodus 14:15-31: Crossing the Red Sea; Isaiah 54:5-*
> *14: The Lord Redeemer will have compassion on Israel; Isaiah*
> *55:1-11: All who thirst, come to the waters; Baruch 3:9-15,*
> *32-4:4: Walk in the way of the Lord; Ezekiel 36:16-17a, 18-*
> *28: A new heart I will give you and a new spirit; Romans 6:3-*
> *11: Baptized into his death, we walk in newness of life;*
> *Matthew 28:1-10 (Year A); Mark 16:1-6 (Year B); Luke 24:1-*
> *12 (Year C): Discovery of the empty tomb.*

The readings at the Easter Vigil offer the paradigm for how the liturgy interprets scripture: the Old Testament passages, proclaimed in the midst of the assembled community bathed in the light of Christ (symbolized by the paschal candle), tell the story of salvation of which Jesus, in his death and resurrection (the gospel), is the culmination. The second reading from Paul's Letter to the Romans interprets the significance of the paschal mystery and explains how in baptism believers appropriate this mystery in their lives. Thus, no matter what the content of the three readings might be, at any eucharistic celebration throughout the liturgical year they always play the same role: the Old Testament sets the stage of salvation history of which Jesus in the gospel is the focal point, while the second reading shows how the early Christians interpreted and appropriated the paschal mystery.

Resurrection of the Lord—Easter Sunday

> *Acts 10:34, 37-43: Peter preaches the paschal message; Colossians 3:1-4; or 1 Corinthians 5:5-6: Paul interprets its meaning; John 20:1-9 (1-18): The discovery of the empty tomb; Jesus appears to Mary Magdalene.*

The joy of the Vigil spills over into the brightness of Easter Sunday. The gospel passage relates John's version of the discovery of the empty tomb, with the beloved disciple, Peter, and Mary Magdalene sharing centre stage. The two selections proposed for the second reading explore the impact of Christ's resurrection on the faithful. The first reading, drawn from the Acts of the Apostles instead of from the Old Testament, establishes the pattern for the first reading throughout the Sundays of Easter.

The Easter Season

> *The fifty days from Easter Sunday to Pentecost are celebrated in joyful exultation as one feast day, or better as one "great Sunday."*
>
> *The Sundays of this season rank as the paschal Sundays and, after Easter Sunday itself, are called the Second, Third, Fourth, Fifth, Sixth, and Seventh Sundays of Easter. The period of the fifty days ends on Pentecost Sunday (GNLYC, 22-23).*

Since the Easter Season is one great Sunday, it amplifies what each and every Sunday already celebrates: the resurrection of the Lord, his victory over the powers of sin and death, the beginning of the new creation.

The Easter Season employs the following combination of principles of reading selection and patterns of reading distribution:

Harmony	Yes. Special books: John, Acts, 1 Peter, 1 John, Revelation
Thematic groupings	Gospels and readings from Acts of the Apostles
Semicontinuous reading	Readings from Acts on 2nd to 6th Sundays; second readings
Correspondence	Sometimes, usually between two readings

Gospel readings for the Sundays of Easter

Sundays	Year A	Year B	Year C	Focus
2nd	Thomas (Jn 20:19-31)	Thomas (Jn 20:19-31)	Thomas (Jn 20:19-31)	Appearances of Christ
3rd	Emmaus (Lk 24:13-35)	The Eleven (Lk 24:35-48)	On the Lakeshore (Jn 21:1-19)	Appearances of Christ
4th	Good Shepherd (Jn 10:1-10)	Good Shepherd (Jn 10:11-18)	Good Shepherd (Jn 10:27-30)	Good Shepherd
5th	Way, Truth, Life (Jn 14:1-12)	True Vine (Jn 15:1-8)	New Commandment (Jn 13)	Farewell Discourse
6th	The Advocate (Jn 14:15-21)	Love command (Jn 15:9-17)	Gift—Holy Spirit (Jn 14:23-29)	Farewell Discourse
7th	Jesus' Prayer (Jn 17:1-11a)	Jesus' Prayer (Jn 17:11b-19)	Jesus' Prayer (Jn 17:20-26)	Farewell Discourse
Pentecost	Gift of Spirit (Jn 20:19-23)	Spirit of Truth (Jn 15, 16)	Send Holy Spirit (Jn 14)	Spirit

Most of these pericopes directly or indirectly describe Jesus and his disciples at a meal, while the Good Shepherd passages on the Fourth Sunday feature Christ's loving care for his disciples. Read within the Easter Season, these excerpts suggest that the preeminent time and place for Christians to commune with the risen Lord is the Sunday eucharist. Moreover, these repasts with Christ offer a foretaste of the banquet prepared for us in the heavenly kingdom.

Readings from Acts

Sundays	Year A	Year B	Year C	Theme
2nd	Communality (2:42-47)	One heart and soul (4:32-35)	Believers added (5:12-16)	Unity among believers
3rd	Peter's sermon (2:14, 22-28)	Peter preaches (3:13-15, 17-19)	Peter's defence (5:27…41)	Peter's preaching

4th	Peter's sermon (2:14a, 36b-41)	Peter's defence (4:7-12)	Paul preaches (13:14, 43-52)	Apostles' witnessing
5th	The Seven (6:1-7)	Saul preaches (9:26-31)	Paul–Asia Minor (14:21-27)	Mutual service
6th	In Samaria (8:5-8, 14-17)	Cornelius baptized (10:25...48)	Jerusalem Council (15:1...29)	Church's mission

The first readings from the Acts of the Apostles manifest a double distribution pattern. On the one hand, moving from the Second to the Sixth Sundays, the excerpted passages follow a loosely-conceived semicontinuous reading, as a list of the chapter numbers from which they have been drawn shows. In this way the Lectionary sketches the first decades of the church's growth and expansion. On the other hand, each of these five Sundays presents the same theme across Years A, B and C.

The tradition of reading from Acts of the Apostles at Easter time in lieu of passages from the Old Testament suggests that the church emerged in history as a consequence of the resurrection of Jesus. By evoking the church's foundation and expansion, the liturgy invites Christian communities to see themselves in the long lineage of faithful witnesses reaching back to the apostles.

Readings from the apostolic writings

The second readings during the Sundays of Easter are drawn from three different New Testament books, again following ancient tradition. In Year A, the excerpts are from 1 Peter because of its baptismal themes; in Year B, we read from 1 John, which describes how communities of the new covenant are to behave; in Year C, the readings come from the Book of Revelation, evoking the final goal of our existence. These readings are for the most part ordered in a semicontinuous fashion. Since each of the three readings in the Sundays of Easter follows its own distinct track, correspondence is not a prime concern; nevertheless, it still occurs frequently. Instances of correspondence between two or among all three readings during the Sundays of Easter can be found on 2A, 3A, 4A, 2B, 3B, 5B, 6B, 7B, 2C, 4C, and 7C.

The Season of Lent

Lent is a preparation for the celebration of Easter. For the Lenten liturgy disposes both catechumens and the faithful to celebrate the paschal mystery: catechumens, through the several stages of Christian initiation; the faithful, through reminders of their own baptism and through penitential practices (GNLYC, no. 27).

The table below lists the combination of principles of reading selection and patterns of reading distribution for the Lenten Season:

Harmony	Yes. Special book: John
Thematic groupings	Gospel and Old Testament readings
Semicontinuous reading	None
Correspondence	Almost always, between two or among all three readings

Gospel readings

Sunday	Year A (catechumens)	Year B (dying-rising)	Year C (repentance)
1st	Temptation (Mt 4:1-11)	Temptation (Mk 1:12-15)	Temptation (Lk 4:1-13)
2nd	Transfiguration (Mt 17:1-9)	Transfiguration (Mk 9:2-10)	Transfiguration (Lk 9:28b-36)
3rd	Samaritan woman (Jn 4:5-42)	Temple cleansing (Jn 2:13-25)	Falling tower (Lk 13:1-9)
4th	Man born blind (Jn 9:1-41)	Nicodemus (Jn 3:14-21)	Prodigal son (Lk 15:1-3,11-32)
5th	Raising of Lazarus (Jn 11:1-45)	Grain of wheat (Jn 12:20-33)	Woman in adultery (Jn 8:1-11)

The Lenten gospels exhibit a particular pattern. In all three Lectionary Years A, B and C, the First Sunday presents the account of the temptation of Jesus, while the gospel passages for the Second Sunday recount the transfiguration. Together these two Sundays form an overture to the entire Lent-Easter cycle by evoking the two key facets of the paschal mystery—the death and resurrection of Jesus.

After this initial similarity, the three Lectionary years diverge, as the above table shows. The readings for the Third, Fourth and Fifth Sundays in Year A constitute a thematic group-

ing oriented to the candidates for initiation. Read in the baptismal context of Lent, the excerpts illustrate what happens when someone meets the Lord, and thus provide models through which catechumens can interpret their own experience of coming to faith. Initiation means passing over from sin, darkness and death into grace, light and life.

In Year B, the gospel passages for the Third, Fourth and Fifth Sundays of Lent present three different Johannine images of the paschal mystery as found in the preaching of Jesus: "Destroy this temple, and in three days I will raise it up" (Third Sunday); "And just as Moses lifted up the serpent in the wilderness, so must the Son of Man be lifted up, that whoever believes in him may have eternal life" (Fourth Sunday); "... unless a grain of wheat falls into the earth and dies, it remains just a single grain: but if it dies, it bears much fruit. Those who love their life lose it, and those who hate their life in this world will keep it for eternal life" (Fifth Sunday).

The thematic grouping for the Third, Fourth and Fifth Sundays of Lent in Year C speaks of repentance and conversion. These gospel readings remind the faithful that baptismal commitment, especially for those who were initiated as infants, needs to be continually deepened and reappropriated through repentance and conversion.

Old Testament readings

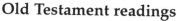

Sunday	Year A	Year B	Year C	Focus
1st	The Fall (Gn 2, 3)	Covenant: Noah (Gn 9:8-15)	Ancient creed (Dt 26:4-10)	Primeval history
2nd	Call of Abraham (Gn 12:1-4)	Sacrifice of Isaac (Gn 22)	Covenant: Abraham (Gn 15)	Ancestral history
3rd	Water in desert (Ex 17:3-7)	Ten commandments (Ex 20:1-17)	Burning bush (Ex 3)	Moses
4th	David Anointed King (1 Sm 16)	Exile-return (2 Chr 36)	Promised land (Josh 5)	Promised land
5th	Dry bones (Ez 37:12-14)	New covenant (Jr 31:31-34)	New thing (Is 43:16-21)	Promise of fulfillment

The Old Testament selections for the Sundays of Lent display a pattern of their own. In each of the three Lectionary years, moving from the First to the Fifth Sunday, the Old Testament passages offer an overview of the history of salvation. This rapid survey of salvation history anticipates the Easter Vigil readings from the Old Testament where a similar, more ample retelling takes place. In this way Christians are reminded that the paschal mystery is the climax of the story of salvation.

Apostolic writings

Like the gospel readings and the Old Testament passages, the second readings from the apostolic writings are also selected according to the principle of harmony to reflect the main themes of the season. Unlike the other two readings, however, the second readings do not display any thematic groupings. Instead, they more often than not correspond with either, or both, the gospel and the Old Testament excerpt. A good example of correspondence among all three readings appears on the First Sunday of Lent, Year A. Paired with the Matthean version of Jesus' temptation is the story of the temptation and fall of Adam and Eve in Genesis 2 and 3. The second reading from Romans 5:12-21 provides a bridge between the other two readings with its Adam/Christ typology: whereas the first Adam was tempted and succumbed, the last Adam remained faithful, not only through temptation, but even unto death. If Adam marks the beginning of the first creation, characterized by sin and death, the risen Christ stands as the first fruits of the new creation whose hallmarks are grace and life. Correspondence can be found, in one form or another, on all the Sundays of Lent in all three Lectionary years.

The Christmas Season

Next to the yearly celebration of the paschal mystery, the Church holds most sacred the memorial of Christ's birth and early manifestations. This is the purpose of the Christmas season (GNLYC, 32).

The Christmas season celebrates the paschal mystery of Jesus' death and resurrection in a different key, underscoring the mystery's infinite reach and universal embrace. It does this by drawing on the winter solstice themes of darkness and light—Christmas celebrates the dawning of God's conquest of the powers of darkness, sin and death. The eternal Word of God, by becoming flesh, by emptying himself and taking the form of a slave to the point of dying on a cross, revealed the paschal nature of God.

Christmastide, unlike the other liturgical seasons which are composed of batches of Sundays, rests on the foundation of two pillar feasts, Christmas and Epiphany. Both are solstice feasts, the first based on the Roman calendar which located the winter solstice on December 25, the second on an ancient Egyptian calendar which celebrated the solstice on January 6. Whether as a Christian way of countering the influence of pagan feasts or as the result of Christian computation based on biblical indices, the fourth-century church began to celebrate Jesus' birth at this pivotal juncture of the solar year. The other seasonal feasts—the Holy Family, Mary the Mother of God, the Baptism of the Lord, as well as the Sunday after Christmas—are ancillary to, and draw their themes from, the two pillar celebrations.

The lectionary readings are selected according to harmony, but, due to the nature of the Christmas season, they do not display any thematic groupings or semicontinuous reading. The particular combination of principles of reading selection and distribution are as follows:

Harmony	Yes. Special books: Isaiah; Matthew 1-2, Luke 1-2
Thematic groupings	The four Christmas Masses
Semicontinuous reading	None
Correspondence	Yes. All three readings at each celebration

Gospels

The gospels for this season recount Jesus' birth and the marvellous events surrounding his early manifestations.

Christmas	Vigil:	Genealogy of Jesus (Mt 1:1-25)
	Night:	Birth of Jesus (Lk 2:1-16)
	Dawn:	Shepherds' visit (Lk 2:15-20)
	Day:	John's prologue—"the Word became flesh" (Jn 1:1-18)
Holy Family	Year A:	Flight to Egypt, return to Nazareth (Mt 2:13-15, 19-23)
	Year B:	Purification, Simeon and Anna at the Temple (Lk 2:22-40)
	Year C:	Boy Jesus at the Temple (Lk 2:41-52)
Mary, Mother of God		Shepherds' visit, circumcision, naming (Lk 2:16-21)
Second Sunday after Christmas		John's prologue (Jn 1:1-18)
Epiphany		Magi's visit (Mt 2:1-12)
Baptism of the Lord	Year A:	Baptism (Mt 3:13-17)
	Year B:	Baptism (Mk 1:7-11)
	Year C:	Baptism (Lk 3:15-16, 21-22)

The gospels do not narrate events in their strict chronological order. For example, the story of the 12-year-old Jesus teaching the elders in the Temple (Feast of the Holy Family, Year C) is read prior to the Epiphany when the magi come to worship the child Jesus. But the liturgy is never constrained by chronology; it is mystery, not biography, that liturgy celebrates.

The theme of the early manifestations of Jesus embraces the entire season. The several manifestations can be identified as follows:

- to the shepherds on the night of his birth, manifestation to the poor and humble

- in the Temple at the purification, manifestation at the heart of Jewish religion

- to the magi, manifestation to the nations

- at his baptism, manifestation of Father, Son and Spirit

These manifestations recounted in the infancy narratives foreshadow the revelation of the paschal mystery and announce the full revelation of Jesus' glory in his return at the end of time. The baptism, a feast which serves the double function of closing the Christmas season and opening Ordinary Time, marks the first time in the gospel accounts that God speaks.

Old Testament

The Old Testament readings are all selected according to harmony, and all correspond to the gospel of the day.

Christmas	Vigil:	The Lord delights in Zion (Isa 62:1-5)
	Night:	"The people who walked in darkness have seen a great light ... For a child has been born to us ... " (Isa 9:2-4, 6-7)
	Dawn:	"See, your salvation comes" (Isa 62:11-12)
	Day:	"All the ends of the earth shall see the salvation of our God" (Isa 52:7-10)
Holy Family	Year A:	Those who respect the Lord honour their parents (Sir 3:2-6, 12-14)
	Year B:	The Lord promises offspring to Abraham (Gen 15:1-6; 17:3b-5, 15-16; 21:1-7)
	Year C:	The boy Samuel is dedicated to the Lord's service (1 Sam 1:11, 20-22, 24-28)
Mary, Mother of God		The Aaronic blessing (Num 6:22-27)
Second Sunday after Christmas		Wisdom makes her dwelling among God's people (Sir 24:1-4, 8-12)
Epiphany		The glory of the Lord has risen upon Jerusalem (Isa 60:1-6)
Baptism of the Lord	Year A:	Here is my servant in whom my soul delights (Isa 42:1-4, 6-7)
	Year B:	Incline your ear, and come to the waters; listen, so that you may live (Isa 55:1-11)
	Year C:	The glory of the Lord shall be revealed, and all people shall see it (Isa 40:1-5, 9-11)

Eight of the thirteen Old Testament readings come from the prophet Isaiah. The four Isaian oracles selected for the Christmas Masses speak of Israel's return from the Babylonian Exile. Read at Christmas, they imply that the redemption effected long ago sheds light on the meaning of Jesus' birth: just as God brought the people back to their own land from the darkness of exile, so now, in the birth of Jesus, God redeems all who believe from the darkness of sin and death. The passage for Epiphany proclaims the universal embrace of God's salvation, as does the excerpt for the Baptism, Year C. In Years A and B, the Isaiah texts express baptismal themes. The remaining Old Testament passages (for the Feast of the Holy Family, Mary Mother of God, and the Second Sunday after Christmas) amplify the themes and images found in the respective gospels of each celebration.

Apostolic writings

While none of the four readings from the apostolic writings speaks of Jesus' birth as such, they all provide interpretations of the event's significance. Each in its own way recapitulates the role of Jesus in God's plan of salvation, usually including a reflection of its impact on those who believe.

These New Testament passages admirably fulfill their role as second readings: they interpret the mystery of Christ and show how the early Christian generations appropriated this mystery and lived it in their lives. In every instance, the readings correspond with one or both of the other two passages assigned to a celebration.

Christmas	**Vigil:**	Paul preaches about Jesus, descendant of David (Acts 13:16-17, 22-25)
	Night:	The grace of God has appeared, bringing salvation to all (Titus 2:11-14)
	Dawn:	The goodness and loving kindness of God has saved us (Titus 3:4-7)
	Day:	In these last days God has spoken to us by a Son (Heb 1:1-6)
Holy Family	**Year A:**	Family life in the Lord (Col 3:12-21)
	Year B:	The faith of Abraham, Sarah and Isaac (Heb 11:8, 11-12, 17-19)
	Year C:	We are called children of God; that is what we are (1 Jn 3:1-2, 21-24).
Mary, Mother of God		When the time had come, God sent his Son, born of a woman (Gal 4:4-7)
Second Sunday after Christmas		God destined us for adoption as God's children through Jesus Christ (Eph 1:3-6, 15-19)
Epiphany		Now the mystery has been revealed: now the Gentiles have become fellow heirs of the promise (Eph 3:2-3a, 5-6)
Baptism of the Lord	**Year A:**	God anointed Jesus with the Holy Spirit and with power (Acts 10:34-38)
	Year B:	Three testify: the Spirit and the water and the blood (1 Jn 5:1-9)
	Year C:	God saved us through the water of rebirth and renewal by the Holy Spirit (Titus 2:11-14; 3:4-7)

The Season of Advent

Advent has a twofold character: as a season to prepare for Christmas when Christ's first coming to us is remembered; as a season when that remembrance directs the mind and heart to await Christ's Second Coming at the end of time. Advent is thus a period of devout and joyful expectation (GNLYC, 39).

The 1981 *Introduction to the Lectionary for Mass* specifies the readings on the Sundays of Advent as follows:

Each gospel reading has a distinctive theme: the Lord's coming at the end of time (First Sunday of Advent), John the Baptist (Second and Third Sunday), and the events that prepared immediately for the Lord's birth (Fourth Sunday).

The Old Testament readings are prophecies about the Messiah and the Messianic age, especially from Isaiah.

The readings from an apostle serve as exhortations and as proclamations, in keeping with the different themes of Advent (LM, 93).

In Advent, the Lectionary selects biblical passages and organizes them in this way:

Harmony	Yes. Special book: Isaiah
Thematic groupings	Gospels
Semicontinuous reading	None
Correspondence	Yes, between at least two, usually among all three, readings

Gospel readings

As the GNLYC specifies, the Lectionary organizes the gospel passages selected for the Sundays of Advent in the following pattern:

Sundays	Year A	Year B	Year C
1st	Keep awake (Mt 24:37-44)	Keep alert (Mk 13:31-37)	Be alert (Lk 21:25-28, 34-36)
2nd	John's preaching (Mt 3:1-12)	John's preaching (Mk 1:1-8)	John's preaching (Lk 3:1-6)
3rd	The Coming One (Mt 11:2-11)	John's witness (Jn 1:6-8, 19-28)	John's exhortation (Lk 3:10-18)
4th	Joseph's dream (Mt 1:18-24)	Annunciation (Lk 1:26-38)	Visitation (Lk 1:39-45)

It is fascinating to note that, through the sequence running from the First to the Fourth Sunday in all three Lectionary Years, Advent presents time in *reverse*. The First Sunday speaks of the final consummation at the end of time, the Second and Third Sundays narrate incidents that took place in Jesus' public ministry, and the Fourth Sunday recounts episodes announcing his birth. By structuring the gospels in this way, the liturgy implies that the meaning of Jesus' birth can be understood only in light of the entire mystery of Christ, from his pre-existence to his reigning in glory. Conversely, anticipating Jesus' second coming at the end of time makes sense only because he was born in our midst.

Old Testament

With but one exception (2 Samuel 7 read on the Fourth Sunday, Year B), all the texts are excerpted from prophetic books, and, of these, more than half (seven) come from Isaiah. Resplendent with some of the most vivid images the Hebrew scriptures have to offer, these selections draw heavily from Israel's experience of the Babylonian exile. The underlying motifs of abandonment and exile, return and restoration, here transformed into the liturgical key of Advent, aptly typify humankind, once burdened with sin and death, now freed by God's mighty act of salvation in Christ Jesus.

Apostolic writings

In joyfully commemorating the coming of Christ at his birth on the one hand, and devoutly anticipating his second coming at the end of time on the other, we now find ourselves between the two events. These twelve New Testament passages from the apostolic writings, true to their role as second readings, help us to see where we are in God's story of salvation by interpreting the meaning of the mystery of Christ. They also provide us with guidelines for how we are to behave in the interim: in Paul's words, we are "to put on the Lord Jesus Christ" (Rom 13:14, First Sunday of Advent, Year A) and to "work out [our] salvation with fear and trembling" (Phil 2:12), resting assured that "[God] who began a good work among you will bring it to completion by the day of Jesus Christ" (Phil 1:6, Second Sunday of Advent, Year C).

The Lectionary readings for the season of Advent paradoxically exhort patience and sobriety, constantly stoking the desire for the glorious consummation of all things. In the name of all creation, Christians repeat the ancient prayer of holy impatience, "Maranatha! Our Lord, Come!"

Ordinary Time

The liturgical year is divided into two kinds of seasons, festal seasons (Advent, Christmas, Lent and Easter) and Ordinary Time. The difference between the two stems from the way the Sundays in each category relate to the paschal mystery. While each Sunday celebrates the entire paschal mystery, the Sundays in the festal seasons have the added feature of stressing a particular aspect of it. The Sundays in Ordinary Time, however, "do not celebrate a specific aspect of the mystery of Christ. Rather ... they are devoted to the mystery of Christ in all its aspects"(GNLYC, 43).

To highlight the mystery of Christ in all its aspects, the Lectionary for Ordinary Time employs the principle of semicontinuous reading. Semicontinuous reading, then, is the distinctive trait of the Sundays in Ordinary Time:

Harmony	None
Thematic groupings	None
Semicontinuous reading	Gospels and second readings
Correspondence	Between Old Testament reading and gospel

Gospel readings

For the Sundays in Ordinary Time, the Lectionary selects excerpts from each of the three synoptic gospels and distributes them in a semicontinuous pattern spanning 33 or 34 Sundays, with Matthew read in Year A, Mark in Year B, and Luke in Year C, as expected. These passages relate episodes drawn from Jesus' public ministry only (Matthew 4-25, Mark 1-13, and Luke 4-21).

Old Testament readings

Correspondence between the first and the third readings can take a variety of forms.

- The most obvious is when the gospel pericope of the day itself cites or alludes to an Old Testament passage. (See, for examples, 3A, 7A, 10A, 27A, 11B, 18B, 26B, 27B, 29B, 31B.)

- At times both the gospel selection and the Old Testament passage relate a similar event or deed. (For examples, see 19A, 21A, 2B, 3B, 15B, 17B, 21B, 32B, 3C, 5C, 10C, 16C, 28C.)

- In yet other cases, the Old Testament passage complements or supplements an idea or viewpoint expressed in the gospel (8A, 33B, 15C, 23C, 24C, 25C).

- Elsewhere the Old Testament excerpt provides background for the gospel pericope (11A, 27A, 6B, 8B, 9B, 16B, 22B).

- Finally, in a few instances, the Old Testament reading offers a contrasting viewpoint to the gospel (for example, 13C).

Apostolic writings

Between the Old Testament reading and the gospel pericope falls an excerpt from the letters of Paul, the Letter of James, or the Letter to the Hebrews. Like the gospels during the Sundays in Ordinary Time, selected passages from these New Testament books are distributed in a semicontinuous pattern. In contrast to the festal seasons, the second readings during the Sundays in Ordinary Time do not correspond with the other two readings of the day. The deliberate refusal to coordinate thematically all three readings on a given Sunday underlines the fact that the primary aim of the scriptural selections at the eucharist is to proclaim the paschal mystery.

Conclusion

Preparing the table of the word requires not only a familiarity with each scripture reading, but also with the patterns—the architecture—of the Lectionary. By employing different blends of the principles of reading selection and distribution, the Lectionary configures each season according to liturgy's needs. It therefore plays an essential role in forming and molding the assembly of faithful into the image and likeness of Christ, "who was handed over to death for our trespasses and was raised for our justification" (Rom 4:25).

In Summary

1. The Easter Vigil provides the pattern for the role of the three categories of readings: the Old Testament sets the stage of salvation history of which Jesus in the gospel is the focal point, while the second reading shows how the early Christians interpreted and appropriated the paschal mystery.

2. The pattern of reading distribution for each season articulates the main themes of that season.

3. An appreciation of the seasonal patterns, which reveal the overarching structure and purpose of the liturgy and of the liturgical year, helps us better prepare our celebrations.

Discussion Questions

1. It is always good to prepare an entire season by reading all the passages for that season. In this way, it will be easier to grasp the liturgical significance of each individual Sunday's or Feast Day's readings. Select a season. How do the readings give shape to this season's celebration of the paschal mystery?

2. What aspects of the paschal mystery does each reading reveal?

3. How do the Lectionary readings help us understand the paschal mystery at work shaping our lives?

CHAPTER 5

Embodying the Word

Upon first returning to his home town of Nazareth after his baptism, Jesus went to worship at the synagogue, as was his custom. The synagogue leader asked him to read a passage from the scriptures. Jesus stood, unrolled the scroll of the prophet Isaiah, read the passage about the Spirit anointing God's servant, and then sat down to explain the meaning of the text. In narrating the episode, Luke relates the telling detail that "the eyes of all in the synagogue were fixed on him" (Luke 4:20). Chances are it was not only the anticipation of what he would say that galvanized the assembly's attention; his way of reading must also have made people hold their collective breath. While Jesus was reading, the people must have sensed that something very important was happening. And so, just as Jesus provides a model for us in finding nourishment at the table of God's word during his temptation in the desert, so also he portrays for us what it is to proclaim the word.

Proclaimer

Proclaiming the word means capturing the assembly's attention so that "the eyes of all" are fixed on the story unfolding in our midst. Gail Ramshaw-Schmidt describes the proclaimer's task in this way: "Your goal as readers is to read the lessons so well, to proclaim the word with such authority, that all the people lay down their folders [or missalettes] and listen to the reading of scripture, and, listening, understand. This experience is a corporate one, and one which you as readers have the power to create or to destroy" ("Dimensions of a Parish Program," in Horace T. Allen, Jr., ed., *The Reader as Minister* [Washington, D.C.: The Liturgical Conference, 1990], p. 57). Something is happening when the word of God is proclaimed in the midst of the assembly. What is it? And how can lectors contribute to its realization?

The proclaimer embodies the word. The word of God cannot be reduced to or identified with the alphabetic signs printed on the page—these are lifeless signs, letters devoid of spirit. The printed letters, words and sentences merely record traces of a "voice" that once spoke. The voice encoded in the text expresses a way of seeing reality as suffused with the saving presence of God. Because liturgy makes present and effective God's continuing action of saving the world in Christ, the God-suffused words of scripture, read in the context of a liturgical celebration, become the voice of God's word made flesh. Through the words of scripture, Christ, who not only reveals but also embodies God's passion to save, is speaking.

None of this can take place if the voice dormant in the alphabetic signs on the page is not awakened. The Lord's voice can be made present to us and active in our midst only if it is embodied. Here the role of the proclaimer is crucial. To enable the scripture to become the living presence of the Word once again, the proclaimer lends his or her bodied self to Christ's voice in the text; the lector speaks the voice of Christ in his or her own voice. Thus, the one who proclaims the scriptures becomes Christ's voice for the assembly.

The Listening Assembly

The proclaimer is not alone, however, in making Christ present in his word. The very act of reading the scriptures aloud before people constitutes the assembly as listener. Oral performance demands an audience which is called to listen, for there is no need to read aloud if no one is there to attend to the word. Oral proclamation creates a presence in the midst of the assembly, a presence which the assembly receives by listening. By letting the sounds of the words penetrate into its mind and heart as meaning, the assembly itself becomes a constituent dimension of the liturgy's ritual way of embodying the word.

It is essential, therefore, that in liturgy the scriptures be read aloud. Although today, with the proliferation of missalettes and with widespread literacy, it would be possible for worshippers to read the selected passages individually and silently in their pews, the result would not be liturgy. Without oral proclamation there would be no embodying of the word. Without embodying, Christ is not present. Of course, everything described here in the oral/aural mode applies to the gestural/visual mode so distinctive of sign languages for the Deaf. Indeed, embodying the word is all the more obvious and compelling in such settings—the word of God dances in the midst of the assembly!

Lector Preparation

What technical preparation is required of lectors, to perform their function well? Three things come to mind: love and knowledge of the scriptures, imagination, and skills for public reading. First, lectors cannot proclaim what they do not understand. They must become as familiar as possible with the passage they are to read. From what biblical book is it drawn? What is the greater context from which it has been excerpted? When was that particular biblical book written? What is the book as a whole talking about? What is the assigned passage about? What is its literary genre? (Narratives, prophetic oracles, and wisdom sayings are not all read in the same way.) Who is speaking in the passage, and to whom? Are there several voices in the passage (for example, a prophet quoting God, or several people interacting)? What was the message in its original context? Why was the passage chosen for this Sunday or feast day, and why for this liturgical season? Commentaries and liturgical publications like *Celebrate!* can help answer such questions.

Second, lectors cannot proclaim well what they cannot *feel*. Most lectors read accurately, but in a flat, dispassionate way. Just about every biblical excerpt selected for the Lectionary, however, is filled with passion—God's passion for us, our passion for God, both of which became incarnate in Jesus Christ. That is why the most important quality lectors must possess is imagination. Imagination allows the lector to hear the voice of the text—the soft and loud, the slow and fast, the crescendos and diminuendos, the peaks and valleys, etc., suggested by the words and phrases and sentences. Paying careful attention to the cues in the text helps create in the lector's mind a sort of "mental soundscape" of what the text narrates. Imagination then enables lectors to transform this soundscape into the other senses, so as to see, smell, taste, and feel the emotion in the text and thus communicate the text to the assembly. In oral performance, the sense images produced by the lector's speaking forth the words written on the page unfold the story the text contains, creating a living presence in the midst of the assembly—a living presence which, in liturgy, is always the presence of Christ.

Third, the lector needs skills for public reading. A good voice, clear diction, proper breathing, sufficient eye contact, etc., are basic aptitudes expected of lectors. Not everyone is blessed with these talents; hence, not everyone is called to the ministry of lector. Unfortunately it happens in many parishes that although few are called, way too many are chosen— many whose skills in public reading leave much to be desired. Good will is not enough. Nor are love and knowledge of the scriptures and familiarity with the Lectionary enough. To these essentials must be added the indispensable requisite of public reading skills. Such skills, of course, can be developed and refined, and well they should be. Even good lectors should not rest on the laurels of their golden voices and powerful lungs. Public reading is not a talent to be buried; it must be exercised and perfected.

Microphones

As necessary as electronic public address systems are, they can so powerfully pick up even the softest sigh that most lectors compensate by adopting a casual, conversational tone of voice. As a result, the word of God is not proclaimed, merely read. There is no passion, only perfunctoriness. In any event, it is always a worthwhile exercise to practice *without* the PA system in order to learn to project the voice, to read slowly, and to proclaim with all the expression the text demands. Having mastered that, it is then essential for lectors to practise with their church's system, for every system has its quirks, every church its own acoustics. Embodying the word is not an easy task. Given what is at stake—Christ himself speaking in our midst— it deserves every lector's best effort.

In Summary

1. The goal of the reader is to read the lessons so well, to proclaim the word with such authority, that all the people lay down their folders [or missalettes] and listen to the reading of scripture, and, listening, understand.

2. The lector embodies the word. To enable the scriptures to become the living presence of the Word once again, the proclaimer lends his or her bodied self to Christ's voice in the text; the lector speaks the voice of Christ in his or her own voice.

3. The technical preparation required of lectors entails imagination and public reading skills.

Discussion Questions

1. Remember the three best lectors you have ever heard. What made them so good?

2. Are the necessary tools for gaining an understanding of the biblical passage available to lectors in your parish or community?

3. Are there ongoing, or at least frequent, training sessions for lectors in your parish or community?

Conclusion

Liturgy deals with the ineffable. Through ritual and symbol it evokes the mysterious, elusive presence of God among us. And although the rituals and symbols that make up our liturgy transcend our capacities to rationalize, they are not impenetrable. That is why preparing to celebrate liturgy remains a worthwhile endeavour. The more we ponder and meditate on the significance of what we say and do when we gather weekly to give praise and thanks to God, the more the liturgy can come alive for us and penetrate us with its saving action.

Preparing to celebrate at the table of God's word means developing an ever greater love of the scriptures and gaining an adequate understanding of the liturgy's appropriation of the scriptures. In liturgical proclamation, the scriptures become truly what they are, the word of God at work transforming us and all creation into the paschal shape of Jesus' death and resurrection. Liturgy is the home of scripture. The better our preparation, the more at home we will be.

GLOSSARY

Apostolic writings: all the New Testament books except the gospels.

Correspondence: refers to the thematic relationship between two or among all three readings of a Sunday or Feast Day celebration.

Harmony: the principle whereby the liturgy selects scriptural books or passages that best articulate the main theme or themes of a festal season or a feast.

Lectionary: a book containing an ordered selection of biblical passages used by a community for the purpose of worship.

Semicontinuous reading: a modern adaptation of the ancient practice of *lectio continua* or continuous reading. It is the sequential reading of a biblical book, all the while skipping certain verses or passages.

Thematic groupings: patterns in which biblical readings are organized within a festal season.

BIBLIOGRAPHY

Recommended Reading

Bonneau, Normand. *The Sunday Lectionary: Ritual Word, Paschal Shape.* Collegeville: The Liturgical Press, 1998.

Dalmais, I. H. et al., eds. *The Church at Prayer: An Introduction to the Liturgy, Vol 1: Principles of the Liturgy.* Trans. Matthew O'Connell. Collegeville: The Liturgical Press, 1986-1987.

Days of the Lord. Collegeville: The Liturgical Press, 1990-1994, 7 volumes: 1. Advent, Christmas, Epiphany (1991), 2. Lent (1990), Easter Triduum, 3. Easter Season (1993), 4. Ordinary Time, Year A (1992), 5. Ordinary Time, Year B (1993), 6. Ordinary Time, Year C (1991), 7. Solemnities and Feasts (1994). An in-depth commentary on the biblical texts of the Lectionary and the prayers of the Sacramentary.

Deiss, Lucien. *Celebration of the Word.* Trans. by Lucien Deiss and Jane M.-A. Burton. Collegeville: The Liturgical Press, 1993.

Hoffman, Elizabeth, ed. *The Liturgy Documents: A Parish Resource, Third Edition.* Chicago: Liturgy Training Publications, 1991. This resource contains the major liturgy documents that parish liturgy planners will need.

Keifer, Ralph A. *To Hear and Proclaim.* Introduction, Lectionary for Mass. Washington, D.C.: National Association of Pastoral Musicians, 1983.

Tanner, Norman P. *Decrees of the Ecumenical Councils. Vol. 2: Trent to Vatican II.* London: Sheed and Ward/Washington, DC: Georgetown University Press, 1990. My source for the *Dogmatic Constitution on Divine Revelation* (971-981) and *Constitution on the Church* (820-843).